How to make a Chrome Extension

(And Sell it)

By Daniel Melehi

Where to Find More Information and Help 35

Introduction to Chrome Extensions

Chrome extensions are software programs that you can install into your Google Chrome browser to extend its functionality. They can interact with web pages, read and modify their content, and provide additional features to enhance the browsing experience.

What are Chrome Extensions?

Chrome extensions are tiny software programs that are designed to improve the browsing experience of the users. Extensions can be used for a variety of purposes, such as blocking ads, downloading media, improving security, and enhancing productivity.

Advantages of having a Chrome Extension

Chrome extensions offer numerous advantages to users and developers alike. They can provide users with additional functionality and customization options, while also allowing developers to monetize their work and gain exposure for their brands. In addition, Chrome extensions can be developed using common web technologies such as HTML, CSS, and JavaScript, which makes them accessible to a wide range of developers.

WHAT ARE CHROME EXTENSIONS?

Chrome extensions are software programs that can be added to the Chrome browser to enhance its functionality or add new features. They can modify the appearance of web pages, automate repetitive tasks, block ads, or provide additional security features, among others. Chrome extensions are written in HTML, CSS, and JavaScript and can interact with both the browser and the web page being displayed. They work independently of the website and are installed and managed by the user through the Chrome Web Store. By extending the capabilities of the Chrome browser, extensions enable users to customize their browsing experience and boost their productivity. In the following chapter, we will explore the advantages of having a Chrome extension in further detail.

ADVANTAGES OF HAVING A CHROME EXTENSION

Chrome extensions have become increasingly popular over the years, with over 1 billion active users worldwide. There are many benefits to creating a Chrome extension, including:

1. Increased Functionality

A Chrome extension allows you to extend the functionality of your browser beyond its built-in capabilities. You can add new features or modify existing ones to meet your needs, giving Chrome a personalized touch.

2. Time-Saving

A well-designed Chrome extension can save you time by automating processes or simplifying repetitive tasks. By streamlining your workflow, you can be more efficient and productive.

3. Enhanced User Experience

A Chrome extension can improve the browsing experience for your users by adding features that complement your website. For example, you can create an extension that adds a shopping cart or a search bar to your website, making it easier for users to navigate and find what they need.

4. Revenue Generation

Chrome extensions can also be a source of revenue if you create a paid extension or monetize through advertising. By creating a valuable and useful extension that people are willing to pay for, you can generate a steady income stream.

5. Branding Opportunities

Developing a Chrome extension also offers branding opportunities for your business or website. By creating an extension, you can increase your visibility and establish your brand in the Chrome Web Store. In summary, creating a Chrome extension has many advantages such as increased functionality, time-saving, enhanced user experience, revenue generation, and branding opportunities. By creating a valuable and unique extension, you can reap the benefits and stand out from the competition.

Chapter 2: How to Build a Chrome Extension

SUBCHAPTER 2.1: GETTING STARTED

Developing a Chrome extension may seem like a daunting task, but it can be an incredibly rewarding experience. To start building your Chrome extension, you'll need a few things: First, you'll need to make sure you have a text editor, such as Sublime Text or Visual Studio Code, installed on your computer. You'll write your code in this editor. Next, you'll need to have a basic understanding of web development technologies such as HTML, CSS, and JavaScript. Familiarity with programming concepts like variables, functions, and arrays is also necessary. Once you have these prerequisites covered, you can start building your Chrome extension.

SUBCHAPTER 2.2: UNDERSTANDING THE ANATOMY OF A CHROME EXTENSION

Before you start writing any code, it's important to understand the basic structure of a Chrome extension. A Chrome extension is essentially a collection of files that work together to add functionality to the Chrome browser. The main components of a Chrome extension are the manifest file, background scripts, content scripts, and any additional files you include such as images or libraries. The manifest file is where you declare all the important information about your extension, such as its name, description, version number, and permissions. Background scripts are scripts that run in the background of the extension, even when the user isn't actively using it. These scripts can perform functions such as handling events or running timers. Content scripts are scripts that run on specific web pages, allowing you to manipulate the page's HTML, CSS, or JavaScript. This is where a lot of the functionality of your extension will reside.

SUBCHAPTER 2.3: CREATING A CHROME EXTENSION

To create a Chrome extension, start by creating a new folder and creating your manifest file within it. The manifest file should be named "manifest.json" and should include all the required fields such as the name, version number, and permissions required by your extension. Next, you can begin adding background scripts and content scripts to your extension. You'll also want to include any additional files that your extension requires, such as images or libraries. As you build your extension, it's important to test it along the way. You can test your extension by loading it as an unpacked extension in Chrome. This allows you to see your extension in action and make adjustments as needed.

SUBCHAPTER 2.4: TESTING AND DEBUGGING YOUR CHROME EXTENSION

Testing and debugging your extension are key steps in the development process. You can use the Chrome Developer Tools to debug your extension just as you would any other web page. To access the Developer Tools for your extension, right-click on the extension icon and select "Inspect popup" or "Inspect options page." This will open the Developer Tools for your extension, allowing you to see any errors or warnings and debug your code. Remember to test your extension on different browser versions and on different operating systems to ensure that it works as intended for all users. In the next chapter, we'll discuss how to make your Chrome extension sellable, including guiding principles for making a sellable Chrome extension, pricing strategies, and how to market and promote your extension.

UNDERSTANDING THE ANATOMY OF A CHROME EXTENSION

Before you start building your Chrome extension, it is important to understand its structure or anatomy. Every Chrome extension is made up of a manifest file, background script, and content script. The manifest file is a JSON file that serves as the blueprint for your extension. It contains important information such as the extension version, name, description, permissions, and more. It is essential to double-check the manifest file before publishing your extension to ensure that all the necessary components are included. The background script is where your extension's main functionality is located. It runs in the background even when the extension is not visible on the page. It can respond to events triggered by the user, browser, or webpage. Content script is another important component of a Chrome extension. It is responsible for modifying or interacting with the webpage it is loaded on. This script has the ability to manipulate the DOM or communicate with the background script. Understanding the basic anatomy of a Chrome extension is crucial to building a successful extension. It is important to keep these components in mind as you begin building your extension, and ensure they are working together seamlessly.

SUBCHAPTER 2.4: TESTING AND DEBUGGING YOUR CHROME EXTENSION

Congratulations on developing your Chrome extension so far! Testing and debugging your extension is an important step in the development process to ensure that your extension works as intended and doesn't have any bugs or errors. One way to test your extension is by using the Chrome developer tools. You can access this by right-clicking on any page within Chrome and selecting "Inspect". From here, navigate to the "Console" tab where you can use this to output messages, errors, and debugging information. There are also a couple of useful tools to help you test your Chrome extension. One popular tool is the "Extension Auto-Installer", which allows you to quickly and easily install and test your extension on your own, or other people's machines. Another tool is the "Chrome DevTools Extension" which allows you to debug your extension's background, content, and popup scripts. It's important to note that once you have released your extension, it's vital that you continue to test and debug it to ensure it's always functioning as it should. This is because browser updates or changes to your extension environment could potentially cause your extension to break. In the next subchapter, we will explore how to make your Chrome extension sell so that you can start earning from your hard work.

Chapter 3: Making Your Chrome Extension Sell

SUBCHAPTER 3.1: GUIDING PRINCIPLES FOR MAKING A SELLABLE CHROME EXTENSION

So, you have built a chrome extension, and now you want to earn revenue from it? What should you do to make it a sellable product? In this chapter, we'll explore the guiding principles of making a sellable Chrome extension. Firstly, you have to understand your market niche and the needs of your target audience. You can cater to a specific audience, and tailor your extension to their needs. Develop a decent understanding of the people you're creating the extension for. Ask yourself this, what are the needs of your customers, and how does your extension meet those needs? Secondly, you should aim to create a light-weight extension that doesn't consume too many resources. This will help you attract more users who are tired of extensions that bog down their system's performance. Focus on creating an extension that is efficient, user-friendly, and solves essential problems for your target audience. Lastly, ensure that your extension is easy to use and navigate. A well-organized interface is a significant component of your extension's success. Make sure all the features are easy to find, and there aren't too many steps involved in using them. By doing this, users will find your extension easy to use, and may be more inclined to recommend it to others.

SUBCHAPTER 3.2: PRICING STRATEGIES FOR CHROME EXTENSIONS

Pricing is a crucial factor that you have to take into account when making your chrome extension sellable. It's important to ensure that you set the right price for your extension, so that you're not undercharging, or pricing it too high that users are discouraged from trying it out. Here are some pricing strategies that can help. Firstly, the freemium pricing strategy is a widely used model. Under this model, you can offer a free version of your extension that comes with basic functionalities, and offer a more advanced version of your extension for a price. This will allow customers to try out the basic version before deciding if they want to pay for the advanced features. This model can help you to build your reputation and create a larger user base. Secondly, the subscription model is another strategy which can provide a more stable revenue stream. Under this model, users can download the extension for free, but will have to pay a recurring fee to access some of the advanced features. This strategy is effective because it provides a steady income stream that you can rely upon. Lastly, you can also consider offering your extension at a one-time fee. This fee will grant users a perpetual license to use the extension. This model can appeal to users that prefer to pay for a single product over a subscription-based model.

SUBCHAPTER 3.3: HOW TO MARKET AND PROMOTE YOUR CHROME EXTENSION

Marketing and promotion are critical elements in selling your chrome extension. To make sure you're reaching the right audience, you have to get the word out there. Here are some tried and tested ways of promoting your chrome extension. Firstly, using paid social media advertising campaigns can be an effective tactic. You can use platforms such as Facebook and Twitter to promote your extension. Ensure you target specific groups of users with your ad campaigns to gain maximum impact. Secondly, guest blogging can be another way of gaining exposure for your extension. Identify some reputable sites in your industry or niche and offer to write guest posts for them. Make sure the content is relevant and useful so that it can generate interest in your extension. Lastly, using SEO tactics is another effective method in promoting your extension. Make sure you optimize your extension's page on the Chrome Web Store by including images, descriptions, and keywords that potential users are likely to search for. Investing time in SEO can pay dividends over the longer term.

GUIDING PRINCIPLES FOR MAKING A SELLABLE CHROME EXTENSION

Creating a successful Chrome extension requires more than just coding knowledge; it also involves understanding your target audience and their needs. Here are some guiding principles to help you make a sellable Chrome extension:

1. Identify a Need

Before creating a Chrome extension, research and identify a problem that your target audience experiences. This problem should be significant enough to warrant the creation of a Chrome extension, and a solution that your extension can provide.

2. Keep it Simple

A simple, easy-to-use extension is more likely to gain traction than a complex, cumbersome one. Keep your extension's main purpose in mind and focus on delivering that value as simply as possible.

3. Be User-Focused

A successful extension caters to the users' needs and preferences first. Always keep the end-users in mind throughout the development process and continually ask for feedback on how to improve the extension's usability to deliver the best possible experience.

4. Offer Value and Innovation

Make sure your extension offers unique features or provides a better solution than what is currently available. This will help establish your extension as a mainstay in the market and incentivize users to purchase or download it.

5. Maintain the Extension

A Chrome extension is a long-term investment in terms of time, effort, and money. You must be willing to maintain and improve the extension to keep up with any changes in the Chrome browser, operating systems, or user behaviors. By following these guiding principles, you can create a Chrome extension that resonates with your target audience, provides value, and can become a profitable venture.

HOW TO MARKET AND PROMOTE YOUR CHROME EXTENSION

Congratulations, you have successfully built a Chrome Extension! But now the next step is to make people aware of it and convince them to download it. This is where marketing and promotion come into play. In this section, we will explore some effective ways to market and promote your Chrome Extension to help you gain more users and increase your revenue.

1. Optimize your Chrome Web Store Listing

The first and most important step is to optimize your Chrome Web Store listing. Your listing is the first thing people will see when they search for extensions, so it's vital to make a good impression. Here are some tips to optimize your listing: - Use the appropriate keywords that describe your extension - Write a clear and concise description of your extension and what it does - Use relevant images and screenshots of your extension in action - Include user reviews and ratings, which can help build credibility - Update your listing often to reflect any changes or improvements to your extension

2. Leverage Social Media

Social media is a powerful platform for promoting your Chrome Extension. Through social media, you can reach a larger audience and engage with your users. Here are some tips on how to use social media effectively: - Promote your extension on your social media accounts (Twitter, Facebook, LinkedIn, etc.) - Join relevant groups and communities related to your extension and share your extension with them - Engage with your followers by responding to their comments and questions - Offer exclusive deals and promotions to your social media followers

3. Paid Advertising

Paid advertising is another effective way to promote your Chrome Extension. With paid advertising, you can target specific audiences and drive more downloads to your extension. Here are some options for paid advertising: - Pay-Per-Click (PPC) advertising through Google AdWords - Using display ads through social media platform - Sponsored ads in e-newsletters, online magazines, or similar publications

4. Reach out to Influencers

Influencers have a large following and are trusted by their audience. Reaching out to influencers in your niche can be a great way to promote your extension. Here are some tips on how to reach out to influencers: - Find influencers who are relevant to your extension and share similar interests - Reach out to them through email, social media or other channels - Offer them exclusive access to your extension or a promotional deal in exchange for them reviewing or featuring your extension In conclusion, promoting your Chrome Extension can take some effort, but by implementing these strategies, you can get your extension in front of the right audience and increase your user base. Remember that marketing and promotion are an ongoing process, and you should always be looking for new ways to promote your extension.

Chapter 4: Submitting Your Extension to the Chrome Web Store

If you want to reach millions of users with your Chrome extension, you need to publish it on the Chrome Web Store. This is the official marketplace for Chrome extensions, and it's the go-to place for users who want to discover and install new extensions. But before you can publish your extension, you need to understand the submission process. In this chapter, we'll explore the steps involved in submitting your extension to the Chrome Web Store, from creating your developer account to publishing your extension.

SUBCHAPTER 4.1: MEET THE CHROME WEB STORE

The Chrome Web Store is where users can discover and install Chrome extensions, apps, and themes. It's a user-friendly marketplace that simplifies the search and installation process for users. It also provides developers with a reliable and secure platform to host their extensions.

SUBCHAPTER 4.2: CREATING YOUR CHROME WEB STORE ACCOUNT

To submit your extension to the Chrome Web Store, you'll need to create a developer account first. You can use your existing Google account or create a new one, and then proceed to sign up for the developer account. Creating a Chrome Web Store account is easy and straightforward. You will need to pay a one-time developer registration fee of $5, which helps prevent abuse of the platform by spammers and scammers.

SUBCHAPTER 4.3: PREPARING YOUR EXTENSION FOR PUBLISHING

Before you publish your extension on the Chrome Web Store, you need to prepare it for publishing. This involves optimizing your extension's metadata, screenshots, and promotional assets to make it more appealing and discoverable to users. Optimizing your extension for publishing involves the following steps: 1. Choose an appealing and memorable name for your extension. 2. Write a clear and compelling description of your extension's features and benefits. 3. Create engaging screenshots and other promotional assets. 4. Define your target audience and select appropriate categories and tags. 5. Ensure that your extension meets all the Chrome Web Store's guidelines and policies.

SUBCHAPTER 4.4: PUBLISHING YOUR CHROME EXTENSION

Once you've prepared your extension for publishing, you can finally submit it to the Chrome Web Store. The submission process involves the following steps: 1. Package your extension into a .zip file. 2. Log in to your developer account on the Chrome Web Store. 3. Fill in the required details for your extension, including metadata, screenshots, and promotional assets. 4. Upload your extension's .zip file and wait for it to be reviewed and approved by the Chrome Web Store team. 5. After your extension is approved, it will be published on the Chrome Web Store, and users can discover and install it. Submitting your extension to the Chrome Web Store can be a bit of a waiting game, but it's worth the effort. Once your extension is published, you'll have access to millions of potential users, and you can start generating revenue from your extension.

SUBCHAPTER 4.4: PUBLISHING YOUR CHROME EXTENSION

Once you have made all the necessary changes to your Chrome extension, it is now time to publish it on the Chrome Web Store. This process involves several steps, which we will discuss in detail below. Firstly, ensure that you have completed all the necessary details about the extension. The Chrome Web Store requires you to add a detailed description of the extension, its features, and its benefits. It is also recommended that you add some screenshots of the extension to help potential users get a better understanding of its functionality. Next, you will need to provide additional information about the extension, such as its category, website URLs, and other technical details. Make sure that you have completed these fields accurately, as they can determine how easily users can find and install your extension. Before publishing your extension, it is important to carefully review it to ensure that it meets all the guidelines and requirements of the Chrome Web Store. This can include checking for any errors or bugs that may affect its functionality or security. Finally, when you are ready to publish your extension, simply click on the "Publish Item" button, and your extension will be made available on the Chrome Web Store for users to download and install. It is recommended that you periodically check for updates to ensure that your extension continues to function correctly and that it remains compatible with the latest versions of Google Chrome. Publishing your extension on the Chrome Web Store is a crucial step in getting it in front of potential users. By following the guidelines and requirements set out by the Chrome Web Store, you can ensure that your extension is not only visible but also easy to install and use.

THE BENEFITS AND OPPORTUNITIES OF CHROME EXTENSION DEVELOPMENT

Chrome extensions are not just useful applications that make users' lives easier – they also open up many opportunities for creating new business ventures and generating income. As a developer, the benefits of entering into the world of Chrome extensions are vast. One of the primary benefits of developing Chrome extensions is the low overhead cost. Chrome extensions can be developed with a minimal budget, making them an accessible product for startups and individuals who may not have significant resources or investment capital available. Additionally, Chrome extensions provide a unique opportunity to reach a broad audience. With millions of users across the world using Chrome, there is an enormous potential user base for a Chrome extension. Another major benefit of Chrome extension development is the ability to monetize your product. You can sell your extension outright, implement a one-time purchasing model, or utilize the freemium business model to gain revenue from either ads or paid features. Finally, developing Chrome extensions can provide a great learning opportunity. While building a Chrome extension, you can explore new technologies, learn about the Chrome API, and improve your programming skills. Overall, Chrome extensions offer a multitude of benefits to developers, including accessibility, market reach, monetization opportunities, and personal professional development.

WHERE TO FIND MORE INFORMATION AND HELP

Creating a Chrome extension is not an easy task, especially if you are a beginner. However, there are many resources available on the internet that can help you learn how to build one successfully. Here are some of the best places to look for more information and help:

1. Google Developer Documentation

Google offers extensive documentation on building Chrome extensions, which includes tutorials, best practices, and code samples. This is an excellent resource to start with, and it covers everything from basic concepts to advanced topics.

2. Stack Overflow

Stack Overflow is a popular community-driven question-and-answer website where you can find answers to most of your Chrome extension development questions. You can also ask your own questions, and experts in the field will give you helpful advice and tips.

3. Chrome Extension Developers Group

This is an official Google Group for Chrome extension developers, where you can ask questions and get feedback on your work from other developers. This group is an excellent way to connect with other developers and learn from their experiences.

4. Chrome Web Store Documentation

The Chrome Web Store provides detailed documentation on publishing and maintaining your Chrome extension. It covers everything from testing and debugging to troubleshooting and updating your extension.

5. YouTube Tutorials

There are many video tutorials available on YouTube that can help you learn how to build a Chrome extension. These videos are usually created by experienced developers and can be an excellent resource for beginners.

6. Professional Development Services

If you are still struggling to build your Chrome extension or need additional help, consider hiring a professional development service. These services can help you build and launch your extension successfully and can be an excellent investment if you plan to monetize your extension. In conclusion, there are many resources available to help you build a successful Chrome extension. Whether you are a beginner or an experienced developer, taking advantage of these resources can be the key to building a profitable business.